D1243438

REAL-LIFE VAMPIRES

BLOODSUCKING VAMPIRE BATS

BY THERESE SHEA

Gareth Stevens
PUBLISHING

Please visit our website, www.garethstevens.com. For a free color catalog of all our high-quality books, call toll free 1-800-542-2595 or fax 1-877-542-2596.

Library of Congress Cataloging-in-Publication Data

Shea, Therese, author.
 Bloodsucking vampire bats / Therese Shea.
    pages cm. — (Real-life vampires)
 Includes bibliographical references and index.
ISBN 978-1-4824-3959-5 (pbk.)
ISBN 978-1-4824-3960-1 (6 pack)
ISBN 978-1-4824-3961-8 (library binding)
1. Vampire bats—Juvenile literature. I. Title.
 QL737.C52S54 2016
 599.4'5—dc23

                                        2015021553

First Edition

Published in 2016 by
Gareth Stevens Publishing
111 East 14th Street, Suite 349
New York, NY 10003

Copyright © 2016 Gareth Stevens Publishing

Designer: Katelyn E. Reynolds
Editor: Kristen Nelson

Photo credits: Cover, pp. 1, 7 Michael Lynch/Shutterstock.com; cover, pp. 1–24 (background art) happykanppy/Shutterstock.com; p. 5 Johner Images/Getty Images; p. 6 Dr Merlin Tuttle/BCI/Science Source/Getty Images; pp. 9, 17 Rexford Lord/Science Source/Getty Images; p. 11 Bruce Dale/National Geographic/Getty Images; p. 13 Kozoriz Yuriy/Shutterstock.com; p. 15 Visuals Unlimited, Inc./Solvin Zankle/Getty Images; p. 19 Carsten Peter/National Geographic/Getty Images; p. 21 nemlaza/Shutterstock.com.

Printed in the United States of America

CPSIA compliance information: Batch #CW16GS: For further information contact Gareth Stevens, New York, New York at 1-800-542-2595.

CONTENTS

Words in the glossary appear in **bold** type
the first time they are used in the text.

VERY REAL VAMPIRES

When you think of vampires, you might feel a chill on the back of your neck. Then, you remind yourself they're not real . . . are they? There's no such thing as a creature that lives forever by drinking people's blood, so don't worry about that. However, there are real animals that need to drink blood to live!

There are three species, or kinds, of vampire bats: the common vampire bat, the white-winged vampire bat, and the hairy-legged vampire bat. They're the only bats that drink blood.

FACT BITE

Vampire bats are the only
mammals that feed on blood
and nothing else.

THE BODY OF A BAT

Vampire bats are small. A common vampire bat's body isn't usually longer than 3.5 inches (9 cm). Its wings are about 7 inches (18 cm) from tip to tip. The wings are made up of long finger bones covered by thin skin.

The common vampire bat uses claws on its thumbs to walk around on its victim as well as to **launch** itself into the air! It's the only bat species that can take off from the ground.

Vampire bats may hop, crawl, or walk along the ground like this. They look pretty spooky!

9

BAT HABITATS

Vampire bats live in warm areas of Central and South America. The common vampire bat lives near farms so that it can feed on the blood of livestock, such as cattle, horses, pigs, and chickens. The other two vampire bat species live mostly in forests. There, they feed on the blood of birds, **reptiles**, and other forest animals.

Vampire bats are nocturnal, or active at night. They sleep during the day in trees, caves, and empty buildings in groups called colonies. A colony can be 100 to 1,000 bats! However, bats commonly hunt alone.

These vampire bats are drinking the blood from a cow's foot.

9

FACT BITE

A vampire bat colony of 100 bats can drink the blood of 25 cows in 1 year!

DRINK UP!

The common vampire bat doesn't just attach itself to its victim. Instead, it lands nearby. It hops or creeps over to it. It uses a body part on the end of its nose that senses heat to find where blood is flowing close to the skin of the animal.

Then, the bat uses its teeth to cut the animal's skin and licks up the blood! Matter in the bat's spit keeps the blood from **clotting**, so the bat can drink for as long as 30 minutes.

FACT BITE
Vampire bats drink about 1 ounce (30 ml) of blood at a time. That amount is about half their body weight!

The body part on the end of a vampire bat's nose that locates blood looks a bit like a leaf.

THIS WON'T HURT A BIT

Vampire bats' actions are so gentle that an animal may not even feel what's happening to it. The bats don't drink enough to harm their victims, but they do need to keep feeding each night.

Luckily for bats that can't find a meal, bats in a colony may share blood with others. They regurgitate, or throw up, blood so hungry bats can feed. This might sound gross, but it could save a bat's life. Two nights without a meal can kill a bat!

Vampire bats' **incisors** are very sharp. They look like the teeth of a vampire in a scary movie!

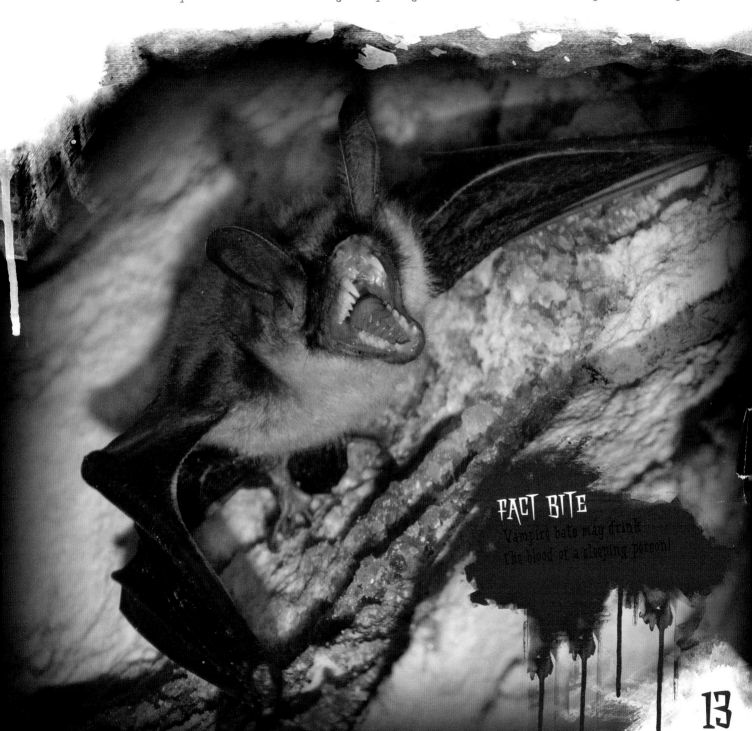

FACT BITE
Vampire bats may drink
the blood of a sleeping person!

BLOOD-SEEKING SONAR

Since vampire bats hunt at night, they're specially **adapted** to find **prey** in the dark. They use echolocation, also called biosonar.

This is how echolocation works: A bat sends out a sound from its mouth or nose. The sound travels until it hits something. Then, it **echoes** back to the bat's very **sensitive** ears. The bat is able to tell the location, size, shape, and **texture** of the object—enough to know if it's an animal with tasty blood!

Different kinds of bats emit, or send out, different sounds during echolocation. Humans can't hear these sounds, though.

TRICKY BATS

The white-winged vampire bat feeds on mammals and birds. It uses tricks to feed on a mother chicken. It'll curl up next to the hen, just like a chick would. The hen will keep the bat warm under her, just like it's one of her children. The bat uses this as a chance to drink the hen's blood.

The hairy-legged vampire lives on mostly bird blood. It doesn't bother sneaking up on or tricking its victim. Instead, it lands right on the bird and hangs from its body—sometimes upside down—while it's feeding!

Unlike the common vampire bat that eats on the ground, white-winged vampire bats often look for prey in trees.

FACT BITE

A white-winged vampire bat sometimes sneaks under a bird in a tree. It then bites and sucks blood from one of the bird's toes!

MILK FOR ME, PLEASE!

Mother vampire bats have one baby at a time. During the first weeks after birth, others in the colony feed the mother blood. Like other baby mammals, the baby bat drinks its mother's milk for up to 5 months. Then, the mother will hunt and regurgitate blood for the baby to drink.

The baby bat sticks close to its mother at first, even **clinging** to her when she's flying around! She teaches it how to hunt. The baby is fully grown by the time it's about 1 year old.

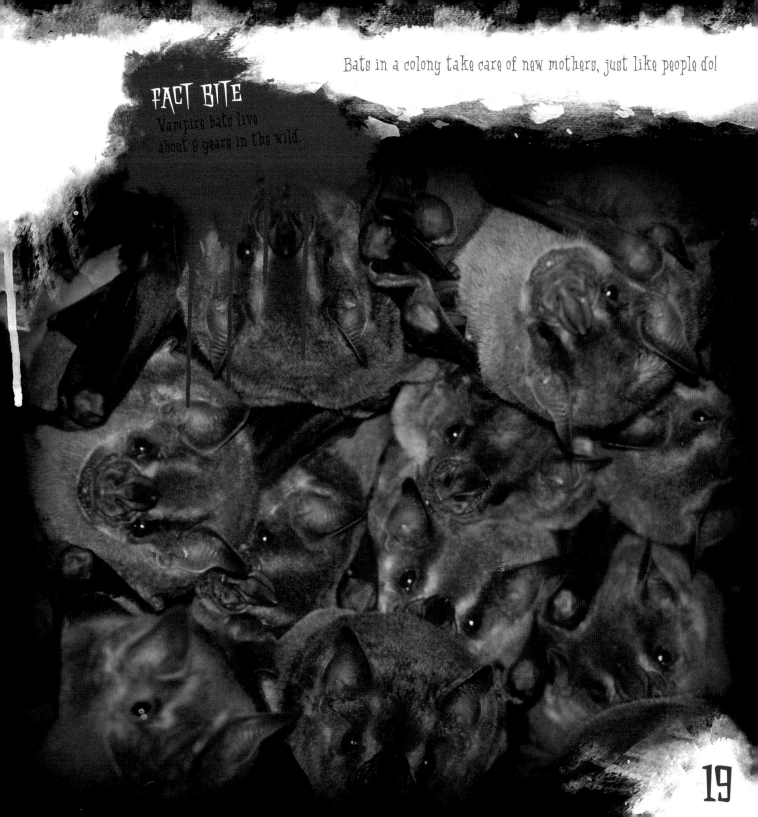

Bats in a colony take care of new mothers, just like people do!

NOT-ALL-BAD BATS

Even though vampire bats don't drink enough blood to kill animals, they're known to spread **rabies**. It's thought that rabies from bat bites kills more than 100,000 cattle each year. There are efforts to poison and trap vampire bats because of this.

Scientists hope the special matter in bat spit that stops animal blood from clotting could help treat people who have had a stroke. This could save millions of people's lives someday. Vampire bats are definitely creepy, but they might do some good, too!

BATTY
VAMPIRE BAT FACTS

- Vampire bats start letting go of bodily waste even before they're done eating.

- Vampire bats have about 20 teeth even though they only need their incisors to feed.

- Vampire bats have a groove, or path, in their tongue to help them drink blood.

- Vampire bats may be able to tell one animal's breathing from another's. This may help it feed on the same animal night after night.

- Female vampire bats may "adopt" a baby bat if something happens to its mother.

- Vampire bats can fly up to 25 miles (40 km) per hour.

GLOSSARY

adapt: to change to become better able to live in surroundings

cling: to hold on to tightly

clot: in blood, to thicken from a liquid into a solid mass

echo: to repeat as a sound after bouncing off an object

incisor: one of the sharp-edged teeth in the front of the mouth used for cutting and tearing food

launch: to send out with great force

mammal: a warm-blooded animal that has a backbone and hair, breathes air, and feeds milk to its young

prey: an animal hunted by other animals for food

rabies: a sometimes deadly disease that affects the central nervous system. It's carried in the spit of some animals.

reptile: an animal covered with scales or plates that breathes air, has a backbone, and lays eggs, such as a turtle, snake, lizard, or crocodile

sensitive: able to sense or feel changes in surroundings

texture: how something feels to touch

FOR MORE INFORMATION

Books

Britton, Tamara L. *Vampire Bats*. Edina, MN: ABDO Publishing, 2011.

Lynette, Rachel. *Vampire Bats*. New York, NY: PowerKids Press, 2013.

Rake, Jody Sullivan. *Why Vampire Bats Suck Blood and Other Gross Facts About Animals*. Mankato, MN: Capstone Press, 2012.

Websites

Vampire Bat
a-z-animals.com/animals/vampire-bat/
Find out much more about these fascinating flying mammals.

Vampire Bat
kids.nationalgeographic.com/animals/vampire-bat/
Read more about vampire bats, including how a scientist trained some to come when called!

INDEX